DESIGN PLAN & CREATE YOUR NEW LIFE

THE ULTIMATE

NEW LIFE

WORKBOOK

The Ultimate Life Coaching Workbook To Create Your New Life

RESET YOUR LIFE

SELF REFLECTION SELF CARE ROUTINES & HABITS
DAILY CALM TRACKERS JOURNALING PROMPTS
NEW THOUGHT PATTERNS
UNDATED PLANNER

Contents

DREAM BIG,
WORK HARD,
MAKE IT
happen.

New Life
WORKBOOK

Welcome

Changing your life and starting a new one, begins with self-reflection. This is where you remember who you really are and what you really expected your life to be like. It can be hard to change certain aspects of our life as life does throw us curve balls and we must change accordingly. But are we handling the growth and changes in our life, or do we need to make changes so our life is better and more fulfilled?

Through the process of self-reflection, you will discover what areas of your life you need to change and how to change them.

Self-care is another important aspect of changing your life. If you don't care for yourself, you will not be able to make the important changes needed, and most often our lives need changing because we have neglected ourselves.

Putting it all together and making those changes is the next step to your new life. This workbook makes it easy to implement those changes and stay the course. Each section contains easy to follow worksheets and a yearly undated calendar to set out your plans, and trackers to check your progress.

It is important to ease yourself into change, as doing everything at once can often lead to feelings of being overwhelmed, so take your time with your new routines and habits as it might be difficult for you at first, but with repetition you can achieve change. Changing your life is about balance and doing the things that really matter to you, so you can create the new life you have longed for.

At the back of this workbook I have included some examples to help you understand how to use some of the worksheets in this workbook.

Have a great time creating your New Life.

Katherine Hay

"Dare to
dream big"

SELF
REFLECTION

workbook

SELF REFLECTION
VISUALISATION

"Honest self-reflection opens your mind to reprogramming, change, success and freedom."

Self Reflection

THE TRUE YOU
THINGS YOU LOVE ABOUT YOURSELF
YOUR CURRENT SELF & LIFE: THE OLD STORY & THE NEW STORY
YOUR FUTURE SELF & LIFE: VISUALISATION

Creating your new life starts with self-reflection. Who are you? Answering important question such as: My Values, My Passions, My Strengths, My Motivations, will help you stay true to yourself and restore the person you truly are, and create the new life you desire.

Reflecting on the things you love about yourself is something we rarely do; we are most often focused on what we don't like about ourselves, and this can damage our self-confidence. It's time to focus on what we love about ourselves for our new life to unfold.

Visualising the new you, and new life you will live, is a great way to understand the steps you need to take to live this life. The feeling that comes with visualisation will inspire you to do the work to make it happen. Use the visualisation exercises to imagine your best day; note you are not expected to do all areas of your life in the one day, just imagine them over several days and how that will look and feel.

SELF REFLECTION
WHO YOU ARE

MY VALUES

MY PASSIONS

MY STRENGTHS

MY MOTIVATIONS

SELF REFLECTION
THINGS I LOVE ABOUT MYSELF

Love yourself and dream bigger.

SELF REFLECTION
THE NEW YOU

INSTRUCTIONS: Topics to cover when writing your old story and the new story you want in your new life.

- NUTRITION
- SELF CARE
- ROUTINES
- HEALTH

- FAMILY
- HOME LIFE
- LIVING SPACE
- FRIENDS

- SPIRITUAL LIFE
- THOUGHT LIFE
- STUDY/LEARNING
- CAREER/FINANCES

- ADVENTURE
- CREATIVITY
- COMMUNITY
- WORLD CAUSES

OLD STORY   NEW STORY

OLD STORY

NEW STORY

VISUALISATION
IMAGING YOUR DREAM DAY

Visualising the new you and your new future, will help you to feel connected to it. You will be more likely to take the steps towards achieving your new life path, through visualising it.

VISION #1: Nutrition; What will you eat, when will you eat, where will you eat?

VISION #2: Self Care: What self care practices can you do and new routines?

VISION #3: Routines: What is your new daily routine like?

VISION #4: Health: How do you feel and what did you do to feel that way?

VISION #5: Family: Are you keeping in touch with family and are your relationships strong?

VISION #6: Home Life: Is your home life calm and supportive? How will you ensure it is?

VISION #7: Living Space: Is your living space peaceful and inspiring? How does it feel, smell, sound?

VISION #8: Friends: Are your friends supportive and do they make you happy?

VISUALISATION

IMAGINING YOUR DREAM DAY

VISION #9: Spiritual Life: Is your spiritual life progressing and are you committed to it?

VISION #10: Thought Life: Are you pushing back negative thoughts & replacing them with positive ones?

VISION #11: Study/Learning: What new area of learning will you start & what platform will you use?

VISION #12: Career/Finances: What does your ideal career look like? Are your finances in good shape?

VISION #13: Adventure: Are you doing something you have not done before, even something small?

VISION #14: Creativity: What creative activity will you do?

VISION #15: Community: What community project or group will you get involved in?

VISION #16: World Causes: What world affairs will you learn about and support?

NOTES

SELF-CARE
and
IMPORTANT LIFE
changes

NUTRITION
EXERCISE & MOVEMENT
DAILY CALM
HAPPINESS
NEW THOUGHT PATTERNS
JOURNALING
CONTINUED LEARNING

Take care of your body.
It's the only place you
have to live.

Nutrition

SELF-CARE

NUTRITION

Good nutrition is one of the most important areas of your life that needs close attention. How you feel will be greatly impacted by what you eat and how often you eat. Low sugar levels or too high can make you either weak and grumpy or erratic and jumpy.

Following a good healthy diet and not skipping meals will make your life better by changing how your body feels.

Plan your week ahead for all meals and stick to an allocated time to eat.

"Good nutrition creates health in all areas of our existence. All parts are interconnected.

Plan Meals Ahead!

Planning is the most basic and easiest way to ensure a good healthy balanced diet. If you don't plan ahead you are more likely to grab for quick food sources which are normally junk foods.
So plan a week ahead and go grocery shopping with a list and stick to that list, so you have the ingredients to create your weekly meals, for breakfast, lunch, dinner and snacks.

WELL BEING   HEALTH   ENERGY   NUTRITION   DIET   PLANNING

NUTRITION
PLAN YOUR WEEKLY MEALS

DAY	BREAKFAST	LUNCH	DINNER	SNACKS
MONDAY				
TUESDAY				
WEDNESDAY				
THURSDAY				
FRIDAY				
SATURDAY				
SUNDAY				

USE THIS TABLE AS A GUIDE TO PLAN OUT YOUR FUTURE MEALS

NUTRITION

DAY	BREAKFAST	LUNCH	DINNER	SNACKS
MONDAY				
TUESDAY				
WEDNESDAY				
THURSDAY				
FRIDAY				
SATURDAY				
SUNDAY				

USE THIS TABLE AS A GUIDE TO PLAN OUT YOUR FUTURE MEALS

The secret of your future is hidden in your daily routine.

–Mike Murdock

Routines & Habits

SELF-CARE

ROUTINES & HABITS: FORMING GOOD ONES

Forming new routines and habits will help you on your way to a changed life. Start with the old habits and routines you want to stop and the new routines you will replace them with. Follow a weekly plan to stick to those routines. Include routines for morning and evening, meals, self-care; exercise, meditation, relaxation such as listening to music, reading, personal care and beautifying your home. Your surroundings will also reflect greatly on how you feel in your new life.

COMMIT TO YOUR NEW ROUTINES & HABITS

Use the planner in this book to schedule in your routines. Use the trackers in the calendar to track your habits and create a natural routine for them. Examples on how to use these trackers are in the back of this book.

"Motivation is what gets you started.
Habit is what keeps you going."

List the habits you want to change and what you will replace them with

Example:	Old Routines & Habits		New Routines & Habits
	Pressing the snooze button on the alarm too many times	→	Keep my phone away from my bed so I have to get up to turn off the alarm in the morning

MOTIVATION   REPETITION   TRACKERS   ROUTINE   HABIT   PLANNING

ROUTINES & HABITS

THE OLD TO THE NEW

OLD ROUTINES & HABITS

NEW ROUTINES & HABITS

ROUTINES & HABITS
THE OLD TO THE NEW

Use the list below to write next to your new habit or routine, eg: the time it will take, how often you will do it and what you want to feel.

NEW HABITS & ROUTINES

HOW LONG WILL IT TAKE:

- 5 minutes
- 15 minutes
- 45 minutes

HOW OFTEN WILL I DO IT:

- Daily
- Weekly
- Monthly

HOW I WANT TO FEEL:

- Joyful
- Grateful
- Balanced
- Relaxed
- Loved
- Happy
- Inspired

ROUTINES & HABITS
NEW ROUTINES & HABITS

	WEEK 1	WEEK 2	WEEK 3	WEEK 4
MON				
TUES				
WED				
THURS				
FRIDAY				
SAT SUN				

ROUTINES & HABITS

MORNING ROUTINE: Create a new morning routine.

EVENING ROUTINE: Create a new evening routine.

Sometimes a workout
is all the
therapy you need.

SELF-CARE

Exercise

EXERCISE: MOVEMENT & POSTURE

Exercise can be any form of movement, and any form of movement produces endorphins. Endorphins are a natural chemical released by the body and they trigger positive feelings. Even a walk through a park will give you positive results. Make time each day to do some sort of movement to not only help your physical body, but your mental health state through positive feelings.

Posture is also another important aspect to consider in self-care. How do you carry yourself? Standing up straight is a great confidence builder, being hunched over is representative of a depressed state, so always stand or sit up straight, it is not only good to reduce back issues as you age, but also gives a sense of wellbeing and confidence.

"A little progress each day adds up to big results".

ACTIVITIES FOR EXERCISE

- Take a walk
- Jogging or running
- Dancing
- Weight training

- Pilates
- Yoga
- Cleaning
- Stretching

- Hiking
- Sports
- Gardening
- Posture therapy

STRETCHING   WALK   POSTURE   MOVEMENT   WELLBEING   STRENGTH

EXERCISE
EXERCISE & MOVEMENT

Choose the type of exercise you will do in your new life. Consider all sorts of exercise such as, walks, jogging, sports, even gardening is movement, exercise at the gym is not the only type of beneficial movement. Give a few exercise routines a try and write below how you felt, so you can make an informed decision on what best suits you.

 **EXERCISE #1:**

BEFORE I FELT...   AFTER I FELT...

MY THOUGHTS, INTUITIONS, REALIZATIONS...

EXERCISE #2:

BEFORE I FELT...   AFTER I FELT...

MY THOUGHTS, INTUITIONS, REALIZATIONS...

EXERCISE #3:

BEFORE I FELT...   AFTER I FELT...

MY THOUGHTS, INTUITIONS, REALIZATIONS...

Choose the type of exercise you will do in your new life. Consider all sorts of exercise such as, walks, jogging, sports, even gardening is movement, exercise at the gym is not the only type of beneficial movement. Give a few exercise routines a try and write below how you felt, so you can make an informed decision on what best suits you.

EXERCISE #4:

BEFORE I FELT...   AFTER I FELT...

MY THOUGHTS, INTUITIONS, REALIZATIONS...

EXERCISE #5:

BEFORE I FELT...   AFTER I FELT...

MY THOUGHTS, INTUITIONS, REALIZATIONS...

EXERCISE #6:

BEFORE I FELT...   AFTER I FELT...

MY THOUGHTS, INTUITIONS, REALIZATIONS...

EXERCISE
PLAN YOUR MONTHLY EXERCISE

SPRING - SUMMER

	WEEK 1	WEEK 2	WEEK 3	WEEK 4
MON				
TUES				
WED				
THURS				
FRIDAY				
SAT SUN				

EXERCISE

FALL/AUTUMN - WINTER

	WEEK 1	WEEK 2	WEEK 3	WEEK 4
MON				
TUES				
WED				
THURS				
FRIDAY				
SAT SUN				

*It's all about finding
the calm
in the chaos.*

— Donna Karan

Daily Calm

DAILY CALM

Finding calm in your day can be challenging, but it's important to find some time every day to decompress. This can be achieved by any means such as; mediation, listening to music, reading, watching your favorite television show or YouTube clips. Arts and crafts may also be your way to wind down from the day. List activities on the following page and work out which best suites you, to find calm in your day.

Try various activities and see which works best at bringing you calming moments throughout the day. Fill the following pages with your experiment on these different calming techniques.

"Rest is not idle, not wasteful. Sometimes rest is the most productive thing you can do for your body and soul". -Erica Layue

CALMING ACTIVITIES

- Listening to music
- Watching movies
- Gardening
- Take a walk in nature
- Singing

- Take a nap
- Read a book
- Arts & Crafts
- Watch YouTube
- Meditation

- Light exercise
- Cleaning
- Day dreaming
- Listen to audible books
- Have a bath

CALM   PEACE   RELAX   DECOMPRESS   SILENCE   CHILL

DAILY CALM
FINDING YOUR CALM

DAILY CALM #1:

BEFORE I FELT...   AFTER I FELT...

RATING

DAILY CALM #2:

BEFORE I FELT...   AFTER I FELT...

RATING

DAILY CALM #3:

BEFORE I FELT...   AFTER I FELT...

RATING

DAILY CALM #4:

BEFORE I FELT...   AFTER I FELT...

RATING

DAILY CALM #5:

BEFORE I FELT...

AFTER I FELT...

RATING

DAILY CALM #6:

BEFORE I FELT...

AFTER I FELT...

RATING

DAILY CALM #7:

BEFORE I FELT...

AFTER I FELT...

RATING

DAILY CALM #8:

BEFORE I FELT...

AFTER I FELT...

RATING

DAILY CALM
PLAN YOUR MONTHLY CALM

	WEEK 1	WEEK 2	WEEK 3	WEEK 4
MON				
TUES				
WED				
THURS				
FRIDAY				
SAT SUN				

DAILY CALM
PLAN YOUR MONTHLY CALM

FALL/AUTUMN - WINTER

	WEEK 1	WEEK 2	WEEK 3	WEEK 4
MON				
TUES				
WED				
THURS				
FRIDAY				
SAT SUN				

"Be so happy that, when other people look at you, they become happy too."

Happiness

SELF-CARE

HAPPINESS

Happiness is an emotional state characterized by feelings of joy, satisfaction, contentment and fulfilment. Happiness is often described as involving positive emotions and life satisfaction. Personal happiness can help you to become more successful in your personal and professional life. Happiness also plays a role in your motivation to pursue your goals, explore new ventures, develop relationships and your overall contentment in life.

Happiness is a very personal thing and will mean different things to different people, that's why it's important to become self aware of what truly makes you happy and positive.

"Finding Happiness can be as simple as looking at what makes you unhappy and changing it to the opposite".

HELPFUL TIPS

Example:

Makes Me Unhappy   Changes to Make Me Happy

Not seeing my family   Plan to see family & friends
& friends often   once a week or video call

GLADNESS   BLISS   SMILE   HAPPINESS   LAUGH   JOY

HAPPINESS
CHANGE UNHAPPY TO HAPPINESS

MAKES ME UNHAPPY: CHANGES TO MAKE ME HAPPY:

MAKES ME UNHAPPY: CHANGES TO MAKE ME HAPPY:

MAKES ME UNHAPPY: CHANGES TO MAKE ME HAPPY:

MAKES ME UNHAPPY: CHANGES TO MAKE ME HAPPY:

MAKES ME UNHAPPY: CHANGES TO MAKE ME HAPPY:

MAKES ME UNHAPPY: CHANGES TO MAKE ME HAPPY:

HAPPINESS

CHANGE UNHAPPY TO HAPPINESS

MAKES ME UNHAPPY:

CHANGES TO MAKE ME HAPPY:

MAKES ME UNHAPPY:

CHANGES TO MAKE ME HAPPY:

MAKES ME UNHAPPY:

CHANGES TO MAKE ME HAPPY:

MAKES ME UNHAPPY:

CHANGES TO MAKE ME HAPPY:

MAKES ME UNHAPPY:

CHANGES TO MAKE ME HAPPY:

MAKES ME UNHAPPY:

CHANGES TO MAKE ME HAPPY:

A positive mindset brings positive change.

Thought Patterns

SELF-CARE

NEW THOUGHT PATTERNS

A positive mindset will help you create a new life. Using affirmations and changing negative thought patterns, into new positive thought patterns, can change your whole outlook on life. Take time to reflect on all your negative thought patterns and write the positive thought that can replace the negative one. Use the following pages to document this and refer to it often. The more you practise these new thoughts, the easier it will be to quickly change negatives ones into positive ones.

Write down your favorite affirmations and again refer to them throughout the process of creating your new life.

"Without changing our pattern of thought, we will not be able to solve the problems we created with our current patterns of thought".

-Albert Einstein

Example:

Negative Thought		Positive Thought
My family is driving me crazy	→	I have a family to love
I have so many problems	→	I love challenges

POSITIVE   THINKING   PATTERNS   AFFIRMATIONS   PRACTISE   THOUGHTS

NEW THOUGHT PATTERNS

NEW POSITIVE THOUGHTS

NEGATIVE THOUGHT: POSITIVE THOUGHT:

NEGATIVE THOUGHT: POSITIVE THOUGHT:

NEGATIVE THOUGHT: POSITIVE THOUGHT:

NEGATIVE THOUGHT: POSITIVE THOUGHT:

NEGATIVE THOUGHT: POSITIVE THOUGHT:

NEGATIVE THOUGHT: POSITIVE THOUGHT:

NEW THOUGHT PATTERNS

NEW POSITIVE THOUGHTS

NEGATIVE THOUGHT: POSITIVE THOUGHT:

NEGATIVE THOUGHT: POSITIVE THOUGHT:

NEGATIVE THOUGHT: POSITIVE THOUGHT:

NEGATIVE THOUGHT: POSITIVE THOUGHT:

NEGATIVE THOUGHT: POSITIVE THOUGHT:

NEGATIVE THOUGHT: POSITIVE THOUGHT:

NEW THOUGHT PATTERNS

AFFIRMATIONS

INSTRUCTIONS: List affirmations that truly inspire you.

AFFIRMATION

AFFIRMATION

AFFIRMATION

AFFIRMATION

AFFIRMATION

AFFIRMATION

AFFIRMATION

AFFIRMATION

AFFIRMATION

AFFIRMATION

NEW THOUGHT PATTERNS
AFFIRMATIONS

AFFIRMATION

AFFIRMATION

AFFIRMATION

AFFIRMATION

AFFIRMATION

AFFIRMATION

AFFIRMATION

AFFIRMATION

AFFIRMATION

AFFIRMATION

Journaling will help
focus your thoughts
and bring peace
to your soul.

Journaling

SELF-CARE

JOURNALING

Daily journaling can help you understand your life better, what is working and what is not. Changes that need to happen in your life will be clear once you begin to write about your day. Keeping a diary/journal is essential to creating a new life.

There are many forms of journaling, such as a daily dairy, a gratitude journal or using journal prompts. Use your favorite journal and begin to document your day and give gratitude to even the small things in life. When you are lost for words on the following pages are some prompted questions you can use throughout your journaling process.

"Journaling is a good way to help us to stop, take a step back and reflect on ourselves".

- Journal everyday
- Journal about specific areas of your life
- Find high quality questions related to your topic, eg: self-confidence.
- Write about your day & feelings

- Journal about the past & release anything holding you back
- Journal about your goals
- Write about the vision you have for your future

CONFIDENCE   PAST   GOALS   GRATITUDE   VISION   FUTURE

JOURNALING
PROMPTS

- What is your goal in the next 12 months?

- What's important to you at the moment?

- What challenges are you struggling with at the moment?

- What do you want to be doing in five years time?

- What's your ideal future?

- Where is your life out of balance?

- What is the legacy that you want to leave?

- What new skill do you want to learn or develop?

- What's working well for you at the moment?

- How perfect is your life?

- If you could have anything, what would it be?

- What are you wasting your time with?

- What's holding you back the most?

- What is your business vision?

- What is your most urgent problem?

- Where are you falling behind?

- What opportunities are you missing?

- What changes should you make now?

- What isn't working well at the moment?

- What have you done so far to improve things?

- What is the most beautiful thing you've ever seen?

- Have you ever been in love? How do you know?

- What is the hardest truth you've ever learned?

- What is your greatest dream in life?

- What's the excuse that you have always used for not achieving your goals?

- What aspects of your life will be impacted by reaching your goals

- Who is your hero? What do you admire about him or her?

- What is the greatest lesson you've ever learned?

- Do you prefer to donate time or money to those in need? Why?

- Do you find it difficult to make new friends? Why or why not?

- Describe the best day of your life. What were you doing and with whom?

- When was the last time you felt that way?

- What would your ideal day look like?

- What's holding you back from having that now?

Develop a passion
for learning.
If you do,
you will never cease
to grow.

- Anthony J. D'Angelo

Learning

SELF CARE

CONTINUED LEARNING

Keep learning in life to sharpen your mind. Some examples are given below. Light study would include simply looking up a particular area that interests you and learning more about it. Learning about those in the past who created great works of art or poetry and studying their work is a great benefit to your life. Learning about those who discovered incredible health services and technology is also enjoyable and makes you grateful for the work they did and the life we now live because of it.

New skills are also enjoyable, this could include simply following a how-to video on YouTube of something that interest you.

The following page list some areas of learning to help you expand your mind.

"Never stop learning, because life never stops teaching".

Benefits of Continued Learning

- Builds new skills
- Opens the mind & increases wisdom
- Improves memory
- Increases self-confidence

- Personal growth
- Enriches your life
- Prevents cognitive decline
- Problem solving

CONFIDENCE   ENRICHMENT   WISDOM   MEMORY   BRAIN HEALTH   SKILLS

CONTINUED LEARNING
LIFE LONG LEARNING

	WEEK 1	WEEK 2	WEEK 3	WEEK 4
MON				
TUES				
WED				
THURS				
FRIDAY				
SAT SUN				

CONTINUED LEARNING

INSTRUCTIONS: Keep learning in life to sharpen your mind. Choose an area per month to research and record your learning in a book. Continued learning greatly enriches your life and understanding. Fill in anymore areas you would like to research and study.

THE ARTS

- Artists
- Musicians
- Sculptors

HISTORY

- Modern
- Ancient

LANGUAGE

- Poets
- Novelists
- Foreign Languages

HEALTH

- Nutrition
- Advanced Medical Care
- Notable Medical Professionals
- Psychologist
- Psychology

SOCIAL SCIENCES

- Disability Services
- Public Outreach

HOME ECONOMICS

- Cooking
- Famous Chefs
- Decorating
- Sewing
- Arts & Crafts
- Designers
- Wood Working

SCIENCES

- Physics
- Notable Physics Professionals
- Biologist
- Animal Kingdom

ENVIRONMENTAL

- Global Issues
- Local Issues
- Groups
- Special Days

GEOGRAPHY

- Countries
- Habitats

RELIGION

- World Religions

NOTES

LIVING LIFE
and
IMPORTANT LIFE
goals

VISION BOARD
RELATIONSHIPS GOALS
MONEY GOALS
CAREER GOALS
HOME GOALS
ADVENTURE GOALS
MAJOR GOALS
NEW PERSONAL PROFILE

VISION BOARD
LIFE AREAS

INSTRUCTIONS: On the opposite page paste printed photos, magazine clippings, or draw and write what your vision of your new life will look like. Remember to include the areas listed below in the diagram.

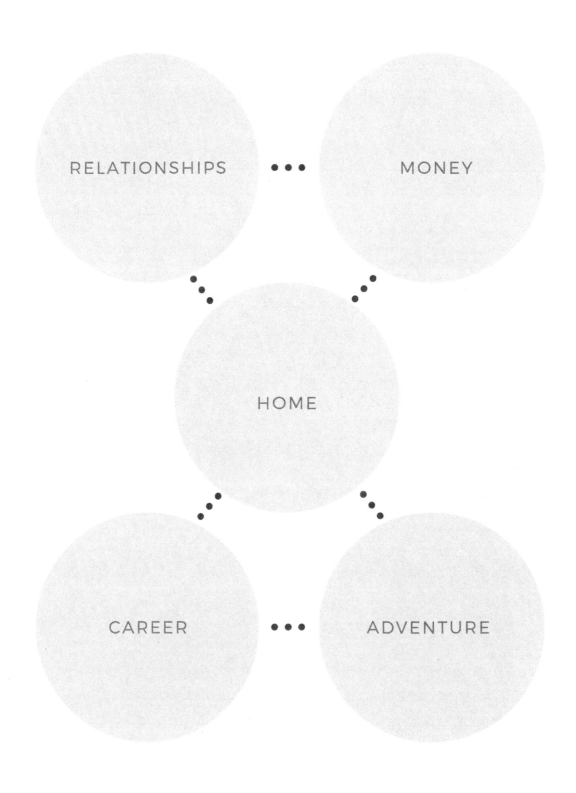

FUTURE

VISION BOARD

RELATIONSHIP
GOALS

The most important people in my life are? List their names, birthdays and special occasions.

What can I do to keep these relationships strong? Visits, phone calls, dinners, game nights?

What new relationships do I want to pursue?

What are my current career goals?

How can I achieve them?

Training/Study/Courses

Mentors to follow

MONTHLY BILLS
DUE DATES

Don't forget those recurring bills, keeping on top of bills can give you peace of mind.

JAN	FEB	MAR
APR	MAY	JUN
JUL	AUG	SEP
OCT	NOV	DEC

MONTHLY SAVINGS
GOALS

SAVING FOR	START	END	GOAL

MONTH	DEPOSIT	WITHDRAWAL	BALANCE
JAN			
FEB			
MAR			
APR			
MAY			
JUN			
JUL			
AUG			
SEP			
OCT			
NOV			
DEC			

HOME
GOALS

How do you want your home to feel? Think of wall color, window coverings, art, furniture, smells and sound, and things you love.

WHAT'S NOT WORKING   NEW CHANGES

ROOM:

→

WHAT'S NOT WORKING   NEW CHANGES

ROOM:

→

WHAT'S NOT WORKING   NEW CHANGES

ROOM:

→

WHAT'S NOT WORKING   NEW CHANGES

ROOM:

→

WHAT'S NOT WORKING   NEW CHANGES

ROOM:

→

How do you want your home to feel? Think of wall color, window coverings, art, furniture, smells and sound, and things you love.

WHAT'S NOT WORKING

NEW CHANGES

ROOM:

→

WHAT'S NOT WORKING

NEW CHANGES

ROOM:

→

WHAT'S NOT WORKING

NEW CHANGES

ROOM:

→

WHAT'S NOT WORKING

NEW CHANGES

ROOM:

→

WHAT'S NOT WORKING

NEW CHANGES

ROOM:

→

ADVENTURE, ACTIVITIES
GOALS

List adventures, activities and experiences you want to do, it can be anything, even the small, from planting a garden, to writing a poem.

- [ ]
- [ ]
- [ ]
- [ ]
- [ ]
- [ ]
- [ ]
- [ ]
- [ ]
- [ ]
- [ ]
- [ ]
- [ ]
- [ ]
- [ ]
- [ ]

ADVENTURE, ACTIVITIES

List adventures, activities and experiences you want to do, it can be anything, even the small, from planting a garden, to writing a poem.

MAJOR GOALS
GOALS FOR THE NEXT 12 MONTHS

NAME:

ONE WORD TO DESCRIBE ME

PLACE PHOTO HERE

ACHIEVEMENTS

-
-
-

ABOUT ME
PERSONAL MISSION STATEMENT

LIFE EXPERIENCES

-
-
-

INTERESTS

NEW SKILLS

Highlight Rating

-
-
-
-
-
-
-
-

_____

_____

_____

_____

_____

_____

_____

_____

Congratulations

Congratulations on finishing the first part of this journal. The next step is putting it all together and living your new life through planning and tracking your goals, habits and new lifestyle.

I hope you enjoyed the worksheets and the process, and change your life.

Now on to living your new life.

Create an environment for future you!

Katherine Hay 🖤

your
NEW
LIFE
starts here

PUTTING IT ALL TOGETHER AND LIVING YOUR NEW LIFE DAILY

Calendar

PLANNER AND TRACKERS TO RESET YOUR LIFE

INSTRUCTIONS: At the start of each month, be sure to slot in your self care routines and habits, as suggested below.

CHECKLIST

- ☐ LOCK IN EXERCISE TIMES
- ☐ MORNING & EVENING ROUTINES
- ☐ CONTINUED LEARNING
- ☐ DAILY CALM
- ☐ JOURNALING
- ☐ POSITIVE THOUGHT PRACTICE
- ☐ USE DAILY TRACKERS
- ☐ FILL IN ANY GOALS OR PROJECTS
- ☐ FAMILY TIME & FRIENDS
- ☐ ENJOY YOUR DAYS & NEW LIFE

Calendar

"It's never to late for a
new beginning in your
life."
- Joyce Meyer

Month:

Monday	Tuesday	Wednesday	Thursday

Year:

Friday	Saturday	Sunday

TOP 5 GOALS

☐
☐
☐
☐
☐

TO DO

☐
☐
☐
☐
☐
☐
☐
☐
☐

NOTES

ACTION STEPS

FOR MONTHLY GOALS

GOAL:

	STEPS	BY DATE
☐		
☐		
☐		
☐		
☐		
☐		

GOAL:

	STEPS	BY DATE
☐		
☐		
☐		
☐		
☐		
☐		

MONTHLY HABIT TRACKER

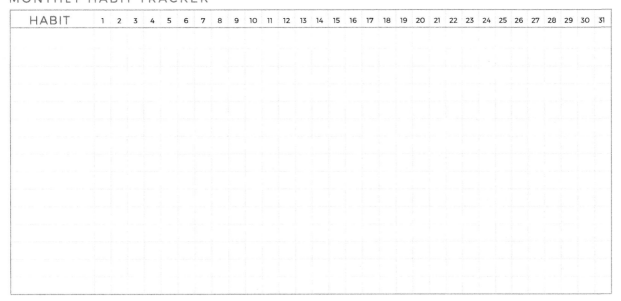

HABIT	1	2	3	4	5	6	7	8	9	10	11	12	13	14	15	16	17	18	19	20	21	22	23	24	25	26	27	28	29	30	31

INSTRUCTIONS: Use the graph below to track areas of your life, rating them between 1- 10. It might be your relationships, finances, sleep, routines etc. Use a different color for each area. Look at the last page in this book for an example of how to use this tracker.

DAILY TRACKER

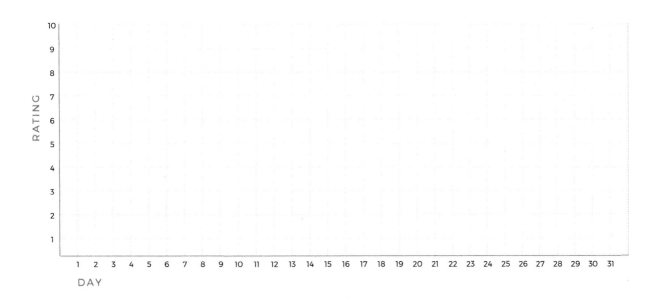

MONTH IN REVIEW

MONTH:

HIGHLIGHTS FROM THIS MONTH

HOW DID I DO? HOW CAN I IMPROVE?

DAILY GRATITUDE

Month:

Monday	Tuesday	Wednesday	Thursday

Year:

Friday	Saturday	Sunday

TOP 5 GOALS

- ☐
- ☐
- ☐
- ☐
- ☐

TO DO

- ☐
- ☐
- ☐
- ☐
- ☐
- ☐
- ☐
- ☐
- ☐

NOTES

ACTION STEPS
FOR MONTHLY GOALS

GOAL:		
	STEPS	**BY DATE**
☐		
☐		
☐		
☐		
☐		
☐		

GOAL:		
	STEPS	**BY DATE**
☐		
☐		
☐		
☐		
☐		
☐		

TRACKERS
MONTHLY ROUTINE & HABIT TRACKERS

MONTHLY HABIT TRACKER

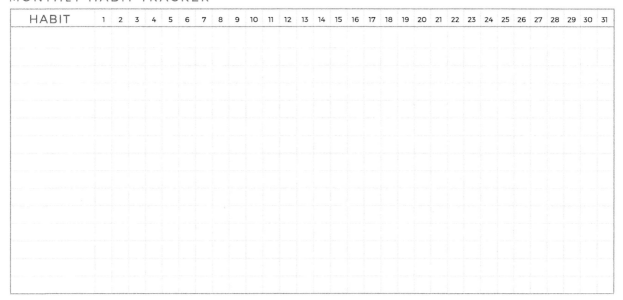

HABIT	1	2	3	4	5	6	7	8	9	10	11	12	13	14	15	16	17	18	19	20	21	22	23	24	25	26	27	28	29	30	31

INSTRUCTIONS: Use the graph below to track areas of your life, rating them between 1- 10. It might be your relationships, finances, sleep, routines etc. Use a different color for each area. Look at the last page in this book for an example of how to use this tracker.

DAILY TRACKER

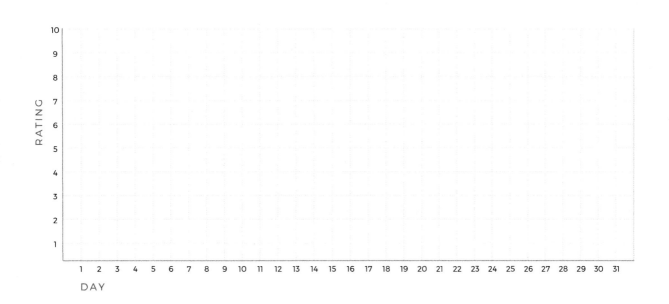

MONTH IN REVIEW
MONTH:

HIGHLIGHTS FROM THIS MONTH

HOW DID I DO? HOW CAN I IMPROVE?

DAILY GRATITUDE

A LINE A DAY OF GRATITUDE

Month:

Monday	Tuesday	Wednesday	Thursday

Year:

Friday	Saturday	Sunday

TOP 5 GOALS

☐
☐
☐
☐
☐

TO DO

☐
☐
☐
☐
☐
☐
☐
☐
☐

NOTES

ACTION STEPS
FOR MONTHLY GOALS

GOAL:

	STEPS	BY DATE
☐		
☐		
☐		
☐		
☐		
☐		

GOAL:

	STEPS	BY DATE
☐		
☐		
☐		
☐		
☐		
☐		

MONTHLY HABIT TRACKER

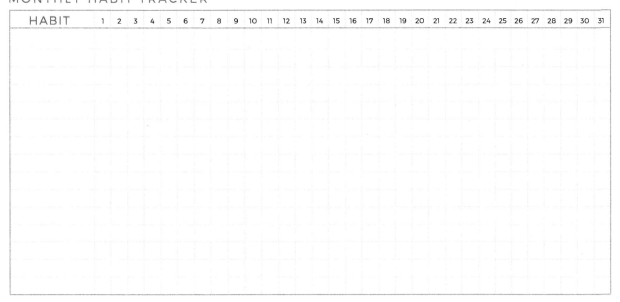

HABIT	1	2	3	4	5	6	7	8	9	10	11	12	13	14	15	16	17	18	19	20	21	22	23	24	25	26	27	28	29	30	31

INSTRUCTIONS: Use the graph below to track areas of your life, rating them between 1- 10.
It might be your relationships, finances, sleep, routines etc. Use a different color for each area.
Look at the last page in this book for an example of how to use this tracker.

DAILY TRACKER

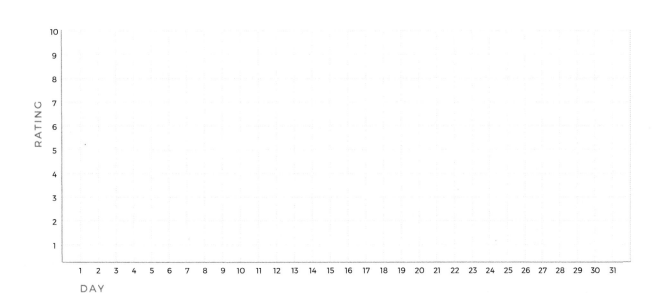

MONTH IN REVIEW

MONTH:

HIGHLIGHTS FROM THIS MONTH

HOW DID I DO? HOW CAN I IMPROVE?

DAILY GRATITUDE

A LINE A DAY OF GRATITUDE

Month:

Monday	Tuesday	Wednesday	Thursday

Year:

Friday	Saturday	Sunday

TOP 5 GOALS

- ☐
- ☐
- ☐
- ☐
- ☐

TO DO

- ☐
- ☐
- ☐
- ☐
- ☐
- ☐
- ☐
- ☐
- ☐

NOTES

ACTION STEPS
FOR MONTHLY GOALS

GOAL:

	STEPS	BY DATE
☐		
☐		
☐		
☐		
☐		
☐		

GOAL:

	STEPS	BY DATE
☐		
☐		
☐		
☐		
☐		
☐		

MONTHLY HABIT TRACKER

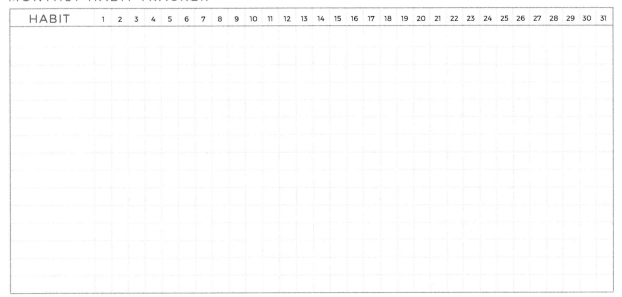

HABIT	1	2	3	4	5	6	7	8	9	10	11	12	13	14	15	16	17	18	19	20	21	22	23	24	25	26	27	28	29	30	31

INSTRUCTIONS: Use the graph below to track areas of your life, rating them between 1- 10. It might be your relationships, finances, sleep, routines etc. Use a different color for each area. Look at the last page in this book for an example of how to use this tracker.

DAILY TRACKER

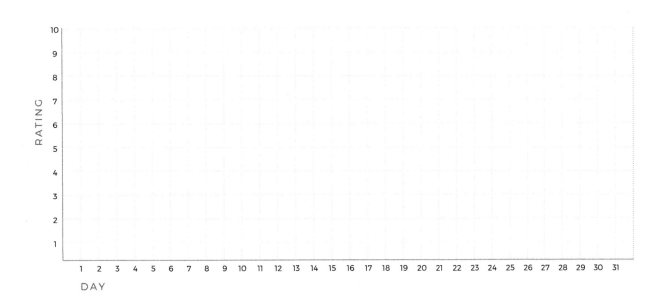

RATING: 10 9 8 7 6 5 4 3 2 1

DAY: 1 2 3 4 5 6 7 8 9 10 11 12 13 14 15 16 17 18 19 20 21 22 23 24 25 26 27 28 29 30 31

MONTH IN REVIEW

MONTH:

HIGHLIGHTS FROM THIS MONTH

HOW DID I DO? HOW CAN I IMPROVE?

DAILY GRATITUDE

A LINE A DAY OF GRATITUDE

Month:

Monday	Tuesday	Wednesday	Thursday

Year:

Friday	Saturday	Sunday

TOP 5 GOALS

☐
☐
☐
☐
☐

TO DO

☐
☐
☐
☐
☐
☐
☐
☐
☐

NOTES

ACTION STEPS
FOR MONTHLY GOALS

GOAL:

	STEPS	BY DATE
☐		
☐		
☐		
☐		
☐		
☐		

GOAL:

	STEPS	BY DATE
☐		
☐		
☐		
☐		
☐		
☐		

MONTHLY HABIT TRACKER

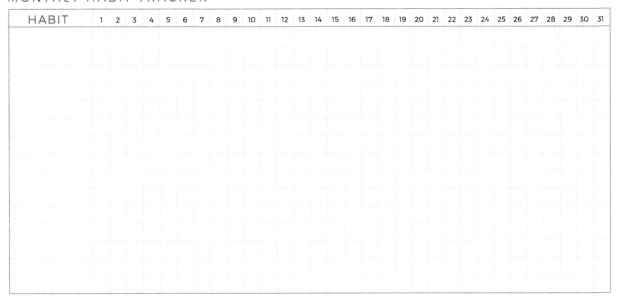

HABIT	1	2	3	4	5	6	7	8	9	10	11	12	13	14	15	16	17	18	19	20	21	22	23	24	25	26	27	28	29	30	31

INSTRUCTIONS: Use the graph below to track areas of your life, rating them between 1- 10. It might be your relationships, finances, sleep, routines etc. Use a different color for each area. Look at the last page in this book for an example of how to use this tracker.

DAILY TRACKER

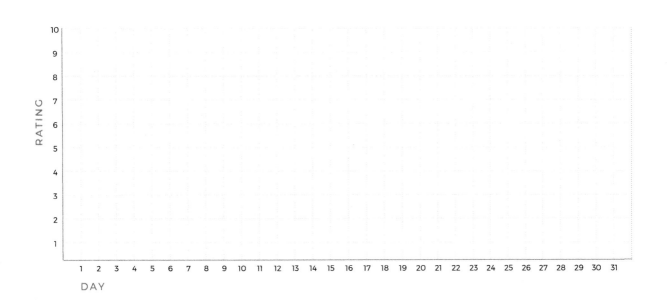

MONTH IN REVIEW

MONTH:

HIGHLIGHTS FROM THIS MONTH

HOW DID I DO? HOW CAN I IMPROVE?

DAILY GRATITUDE

A LINE A DAY OF GRATITUDE

Month:

Monday	Tuesday	Wednesday	Thursday

Year:

Friday	Saturday	Sunday

TOP 5 GOALS

☐

☐

☐

☐

☐

TO DO

☐

☐

☐

☐

☐

☐

☐

☐

NOTES

ACTION STEPS

FOR MONTHLY GOALS

GOAL:

	STEPS	BY DATE
☐		
☐		
☐		
☐		
☐		
☐		

GOAL:

	STEPS	BY DATE
☐		
☐		
☐		
☐		
☐		
☐		

MONTHLY HABIT TRACKER

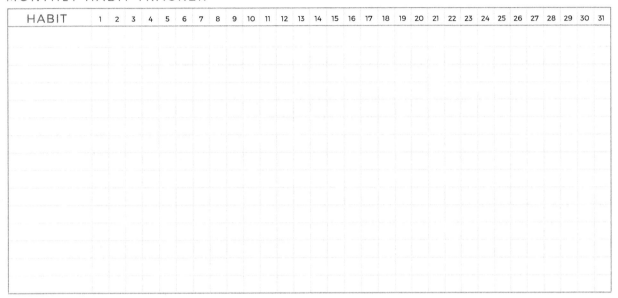

HABIT	1	2	3	4	5	6	7	8	9	10	11	12	13	14	15	16	17	18	19	20	21	22	23	24	25	26	27	28	29	30	31

INSTRUCTIONS: Use the graph below to track areas of your life, rating them between 1- 10. It might be your relationships, finances, sleep, routines etc. Use a different color for each area. Look at the last page in this book for an example of how to use this tracker.

DAILY TRACKER

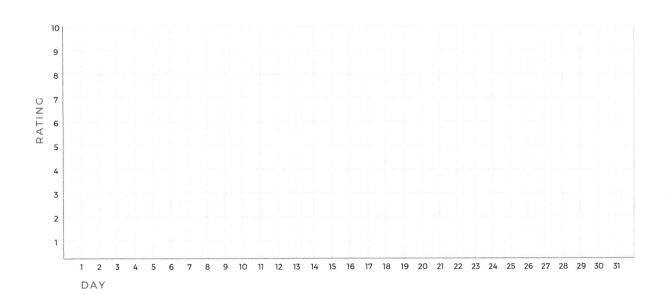

MONTH IN REVIEW

MONTH:

HIGHLIGHTS FROM THIS MONTH

HOW DID I DO? HOW CAN I IMPROVE?

DAILY GRATITUDE

A LINE A DAY OF GRATITUDE

Month:

Monday	Tuesday	Wednesday	Thursday

Year:

Friday	Saturday	Sunday

TOP 5 GOALS

- ☐
- ☐
- ☐
- ☐
- ☐

TO DO

- ☐
- ☐
- ☐
- ☐
- ☐
- ☐
- ☐
- ☐
- ☐

NOTES

ACTION STEPS
FOR MONTHLY GOALS

GOAL:

	STEPS	BY DATE
☐		
☐		
☐		
☐		
☐		
☐		

GOAL:

	STEPS	BY DATE
☐		
☐		
☐		
☐		
☐		
☐		

MONTHLY HABIT TRACKER

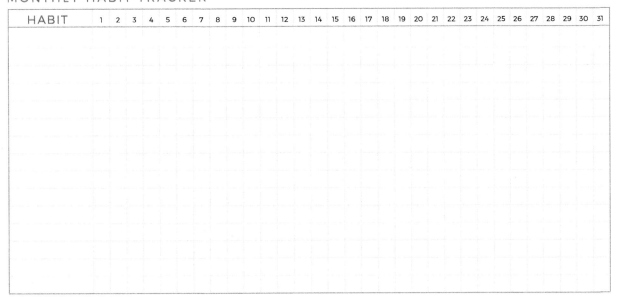

HABIT	1	2	3	4	5	6	7	8	9	10	11	12	13	14	15	16	17	18	19	20	21	22	23	24	25	26	27	28	29	30	31

INSTRUCTIONS: Use the graph below to track areas of your life, rating them between 1- 10.
It might be your relationships, finances, sleep, routines etc. Use a different color for each area.
Look at the last page in this book for an example of how to use this tracker.

DAILY TRACKER

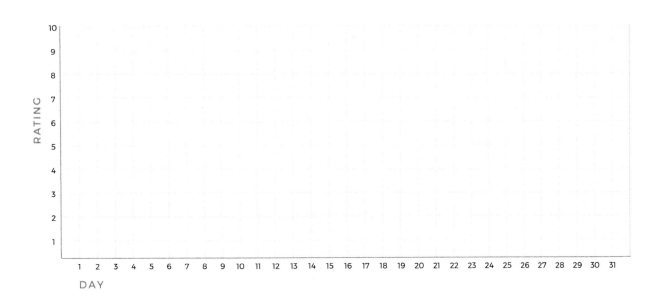

RATING

10
9
8
7
6
5
4
3
2
1

1 2 3 4 5 6 7 8 9 10 11 12 13 14 15 16 17 18 19 20 21 22 23 24 25 26 27 28 29 30 31

DAY

MONTH IN REVIEW

MONTH:

HIGHLIGHTS FROM THIS MONTH

HOW DID I DO? HOW CAN I IMPROVE?

DAILY GRATITUDE

A LINE A DAY OF GRATITUDE

Month:

Monday	Tuesday	Wednesday	Thursday

Year:

Friday	Saturday	Sunday

TOP 5 GOALS

- [ ]
- [ ]
- [ ]
- [ ]
- [ ]

TO DO

- [ ]
- [ ]
- [ ]
- [ ]
- [ ]
- [ ]
- [ ]
- [ ]
- [ ]

NOTES

ACTION STEPS
FOR MONTHLY GOALS

GOAL:

	STEPS	BY DATE
☐		
☐		
☐		
☐		
☐		
☐		

GOAL:

	STEPS	BY DATE
☐		
☐		
☐		
☐		
☐		
☐		

TRACKERS

MONTHLY HABIT TRACKER

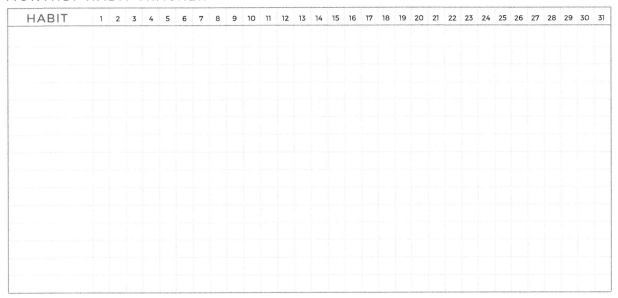

HABIT	1	2	3	4	5	6	7	8	9	10	11	12	13	14	15	16	17	18	19	20	21	22	23	24	25	26	27	28	29	30	31

INSTRUCTIONS: Use the graph below to track areas of your life, rating them between 1- 10. It might be your relationships, finances, sleep, routines etc. Use a different color for each area. Look at the last page in this book for an example of how to use this tracker.

DAILY TRACKER

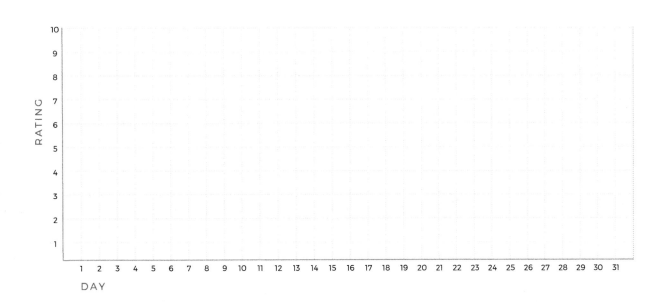

RATING

DAY

MONTH IN REVIEW

MONTH:

HIGHLIGHTS FROM THIS MONTH

HOW DID I DO? HOW CAN I IMPROVE?

DAILY GRATITUDE

A LINE A DAY OF GRATITUDE

Month:

Monday	Tuesday	Wednesday	Thursday

Year:

Friday	Saturday	Sunday

TOP 5 GOALS

☐
☐
☐
☐
☐

TO DO

☐
☐
☐
☐
☐
☐
☐
☐
☐

NOTES

ACTION STEPS
FOR MONTHLY GOALS

GOAL:

	STEPS	BY DATE
☐		
☐		
☐		
☐		
☐		
☐		

GOAL:

	STEPS	BY DATE
☐		
☐		
☐		
☐		
☐		
☐		

MONTHLY HABIT TRACKER

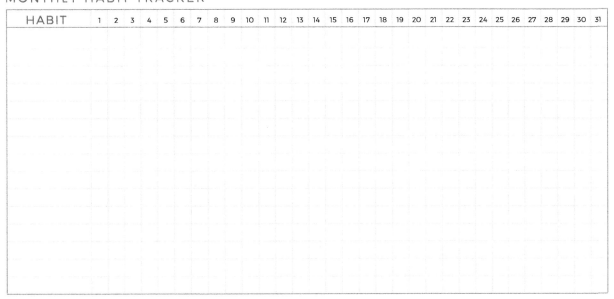

HABIT	1	2	3	4	5	6	7	8	9	10	11	12	13	14	15	16	17	18	19	20	21	22	23	24	25	26	27	28	29	30	31

INSTRUCTIONS: Use the graph below to track areas of your life, rating them between 1- 10. It might be your relationships, finances, sleep, routines etc. Use a different color for each area. Look at the last page in this book for an example of how to use this tracker.

DAILY TRACKER

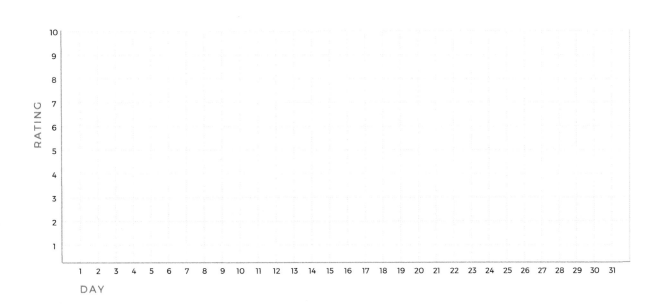

MONTH IN REVIEW
MONTH:

HIGHLIGHTS FROM THIS MONTH

HOW DID I DO? HOW CAN I IMPROVE?

DAILY GRATITUDE
A LINE A DAY OF GRATITUDE

Month:

Monday	Tuesday	Wednesday	Thursday

Year:

Friday	Saturday	Sunday

TOP 5 GOALS

☐
☐
☐
☐
☐

TO DO

☐
☐
☐
☐
☐
☐
☐
☐
☐

NOTES

ACTION STEPS
FOR MONTHLY GOALS

GOAL:

	STEPS	BY DATE
☐		
☐		
☐		
☐		
☐		
☐		

GOAL:

	STEPS	BY DATE
☐		
☐		
☐		
☐		
☐		
☐		

MONTHLY HABIT TRACKER

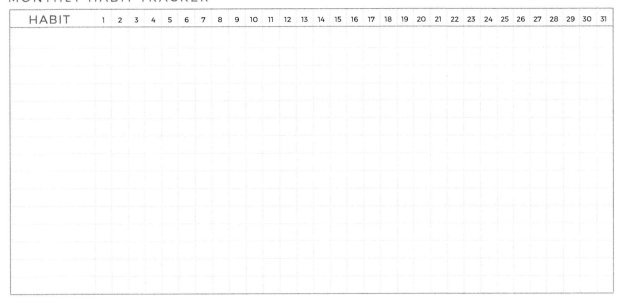

HABIT	1	2	3	4	5	6	7	8	9	10	11	12	13	14	15	16	17	18	19	20	21	22	23	24	25	26	27	28	29	30	31

INSTRUCTIONS: Use the graph below to track areas of your life, rating them between 1- 10. It might be your relationships, finances, sleep, routines etc. Use a different color for each area. Look at the last page in this book for an example of how to use this tracker.

DAILY TRACKER

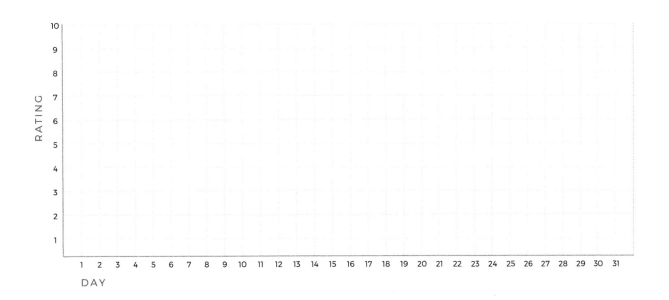

MONTH IN REVIEW

MONTH:

HIGHLIGHTS FROM THIS MONTH

HOW DID I DO? HOW CAN I IMPROVE?

DAILY GRATITUDE

A LINE A DAY OF GRATITUDE

Month:

Monday	Tuesday	Wednesday	Thursday

Year:

Friday	Saturday	Sunday

TOP 5 GOALS

- [ ]
- [ ]
- [ ]
- [ ]
- [ ]

TO DO

- [ ]
- [ ]
- [ ]
- [ ]
- [ ]
- [ ]
- [ ]
- [ ]
- [ ]

NOTES

ACTION STEPS
FOR MONTHLY GOALS

GOAL:

	STEPS	BY DATE
☐		
☐		
☐		
☐		
☐		
☐		

GOAL:

	STEPS	BY DATE
☐		
☐		
☐		
☐		
☐		
☐		

MONTHLY HABIT TRACKER

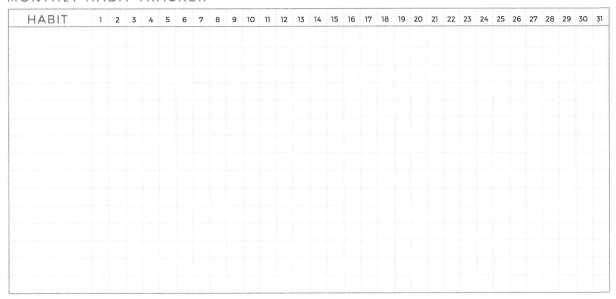

HABIT	1	2	3	4	5	6	7	8	9	10	11	12	13	14	15	16	17	18	19	20	21	22	23	24	25	26	27	28	29	30	31

INSTRUCTIONS: Use the graph below to track areas of your life, rating them between 1- 10. It might be your relationships, finances, sleep, routines etc. Use a different color for each area. Look at the last page in this book for an example of how to use this tracker.

DAILY TRACKER

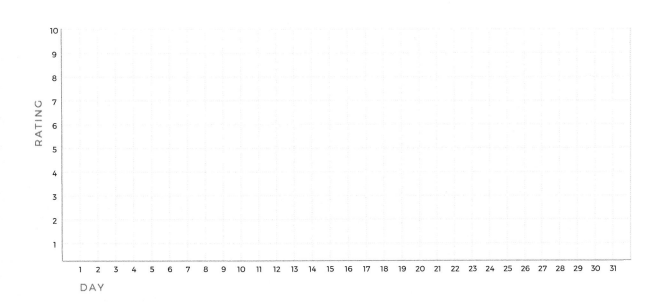

MONTH IN REVIEW

MONTH:

HIGHLIGHTS FROM THIS MONTH

HOW DID I DO? HOW CAN I IMPROVE?

DAILY GRATITUDE
A LINE A DAY OF GRATITUDE

Month:

Monday	Tuesday	Wednesday	Thursday

Year:

Friday	Saturday	Sunday

TOP 5 GOALS

- [ ]
- [ ]
- [ ]
- [ ]
- [ ]

TO DO

- [ ]
- [ ]
- [ ]
- [ ]
- [ ]
- [ ]
- [ ]
- [ ]
- [ ]

NOTES

ACTION STEPS
FOR MONTHLY GOALS

GOAL:

	STEPS	BY DATE
☐		
☐		
☐		
☐		
☐		
☐		

GOAL:

	STEPS	BY DATE
☐		
☐		
☐		
☐		
☐		
☐		

MONTHLY HABIT TRACKER

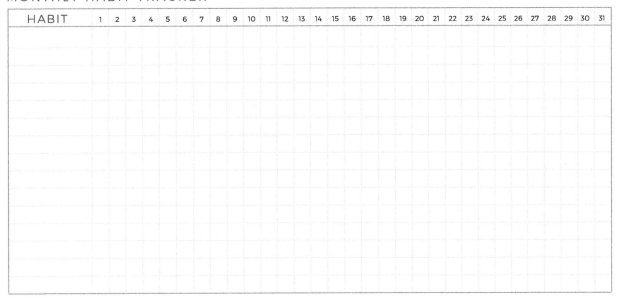

INSTRUCTIONS: Use the graph below to track areas of your life, rating them between 1- 10. It might be your relationships, finances, sleep, routines etc. Use a different color for each area. Look at the last page in this book for an example of how to use this tracker.

DAILY TRACKER

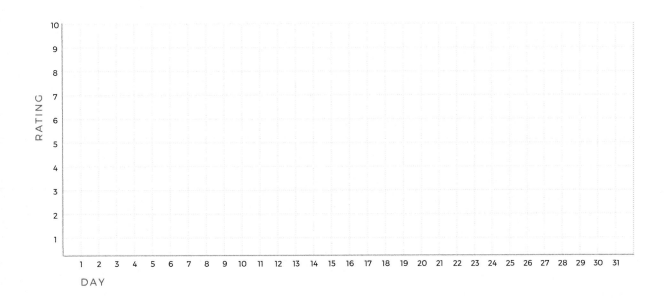

MONTH IN REVIEW

MONTH:

HIGHLIGHTS FROM THIS MONTH

HOW DID I DO? HOW CAN I IMPROVE?

DAILY GRATITUDE

A LINE A DAY OF GRATITUDE

YEAR IN REVIEW

YEAR:

HIGHLIGHTS FROM THE YEAR

HOW DID I DO? HOW CAN I IMPROVE?

YEAR IN REVIEW

YEAR:

WHAT WINS AM I PROUD OF?

HOW HAVE I GROWN IN THE PAST YEAR?

NOTES

NOTES

NOTES

NOTES

NOTES

THE FUTURE BELONGS TO THOSE WHO BELIEVE IN THE BEAUTY OF THEIR DREAMS.

ELEANOR ROOSEVELT

Some examples of how to fill in the pages.

SELF REFLECTION
WHO YOU ARE

MY VALUES	MY PASSIONS
Honesty	Art
Compassion	Charity
Respect of others	Cooking

MY STRENGTHS	MY MOTIVATIONS
Creativity	Family
Dedicated	Self improvement
Fast learner	Emotional freedom

SELF REFLECTION
THINGS I LOVE ABOUT MYSELF

- I think of other peoples struggles and don't judge them
- I am a good friend
- I am a kind person
- I love my brown eyes
- I am grateful everyday

SELF REFLECTION
THE NEW YOU

INSTRUCTIONS: Topics to cover when writing your old story and the new story you want in your new life.

- NUTRITION
- SELF CARE
- ROUTINES
- HEALTH
- FAMILY
- HOME LIFE
- LIVING SPACE
- FRIENDS
- SPIRITUAL LIFE
- THOUGHT LIFE
- STUDY/LEARNING
- CAREER/FINANCES
- ADVENTURE
- CREATIVITY
- COMMUNITY
- WORLD CAUSES

OLD STORY	NEW STORY
I don't take time to relax	I will make time to relax
I think to much about past hurts & losses	The past is over & a new future is coming

ROUTINES & HABITS
THE OLD TO THE NEW

OLD ROUTINES & HABITS	NEW ROUTINES & HABITS
• I don't take time to relax	• A set time everyday to relax for 20 minutes minimum
• Stop hitting the snooze button	• Get to bed early, have phone alarm away from bed so I have to get up to stop alarm

EXERCISE
EXERCISE & MOVEMENT

Choose the type of exercise you will do in your new life. Consider all sorts of exercise such as, walks jogging, sports, even gardening is movement, exercise at the gym is not the only type of beneficial movement. Give a few exercise routines a try and write below how you felt, so you can make an informed decision on what best suits you.

EXERCISE #1: 30 minute walk

BEFORE I FELT...	AFTER I FELT...
Unmotivated	Happy, inspired, creative

MY THOUGHTS, INTUITIONS, REALIZATIONS...
The walk made me feel joy & inspired. I wanted to get back & start on my craft project as I seem to have thought of more creative ideas. A walk does help in many ways.

DAILY CALM
FINDING YOUR CALM

RATE BETWEEN 1-10 HOW IT MADE YOU FEEL (HAPPY OR SAD)

DAILY CALM #1: Sit & listen to music

BEFORE I FELT...	AFTER I FELT...
Anxious	Calm & peaceful

RATING

| 10 | 0 | 30 minutes |

NEW THOUGHT PATTERNS
NEW POSITIVE THOUGHTS

INSTRUCTIONS: Refer back to this list often.

NEGATIVE THOUGHT:

I can't do this

POSITIVE THOUGHT:

I have done this before I can do it again

NEGATIVE THOUGHT:

My family is driving me crazy

POSITIVE THOUGHT:

I have a family to love

NEGATIVE THOUGHT:

I'm not good enough

POSITIVE THOUGHT:

I trust myself to succeed

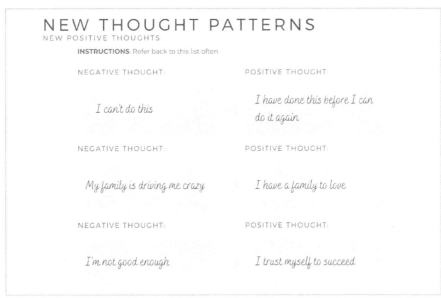

Example

MONTHLY HABIT TRACKER

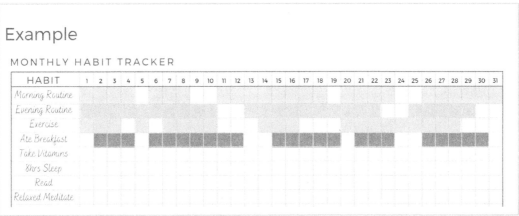

Example

INSTRUCTIONS: Use the graph below to track areas of your life, rating them between 1- 10.
It might be your relationships, finances, sleep, routines etc. Use a different color for each area.

This chart may help you see the relationship between a good nights sleep and what you did that day eg: exercise, morning routine or poor health or overworked etc, It can help you to know what changes to make for a better outcomes.

DAILY TRACKER

Example, remember to think about things you want to see in your life and anything that inspires you.

VISION BOARD

Declutter & redecorate home

Travel somewhere warm for vacation

Date night 2 x a month

Improve fitness

Learn a new craft

DREAM BIG, WORK HARD, MAKE IT happen.

Try a brand new hairstyle

Camp & hike national parks

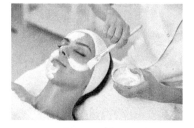
More self-care

Meditate

Eat healthy

TODAY IS A GOOD DAY TO START YOUR NEW LIFE

enjoy every moment.

There are so many beautiful reasons to be happy

Create a new morning & evening routine

Save for a new car

Take some online classes in photography

believe

POSITIVE VIBES

Printed in Great Britain
by Amazon

82622406R00093